Missing Her

Claudia Keelan

New Issues Poetry & Prose

A Green Rose Book

New Issues Poetry & Prose
The College of Arts and Sciences
Western Michigan University
Kalamazoo, Michigan 49008

First Edition, 2009.

ISBN-10   1-930974-86-8 (paperbound)
ISBN-13   978-1-930974-86-9 (paperbound)

Library of Congress Cataloging-in-Publication Data:
Keelan, Claudia.
Missing Her/Claudia Keelan
Library of Congress Control Number: 2009924366

Art Direction: Tricia Hennessy
Design: Whitney Goodell
Production: Paul Sizer
                   The Design Center, Frostic School of Art
                   College of Fine Arts
                   Western Michigan University

Missing Her

Claudia Keelan

New Issues

WESTERN MICHIGAN UNIVERSITY

811.54
K

Missing Her

Also by Claudia Keelan

Refinery
The Secularist
Utopic
Of & Among There Was A Locus(t)
The Devotion Field

To Ben and Lucie

Contents

The Truth is Always Experimentall.

—Gerrard Winstanley

Came Capsizing   the Human Boat

Came capsizing   the human boat

    Came lost   A war-bird's face I wore

    Stolen by drowning

We were an exodus

    Repeatedly in your airwaves

    Once I had a name

    Lost it   with my bird

    Capsizing beneath your heavens

Our own gods lost in the passage

    Your heaven was global

It was full of images

    The earth was one of them

The earth seen from space

    Still beautiful   Unreal as it was

In the pictures   Caribbean blue Ionian white

    A ball you could hold in your hand

And they did   The companies who bought her

I died I guess free   Listening to a machine's whine

Somewhere above me

I. Little Elegies

. . . woman on the grass, your long black hair is crowned
with flowers . . . holy mother, now you smile on your love,
your world is born anew . . .

—Allen Ginsberg, from *Kaddish*

Little Elegy (1977-1991)

The world was strong
The world was very strong
The peregrine gnashed
In the peregrination's dreams
Words in the hallways
Your cough is a machine
Imagine, she's finally a sexy teenager
At 46, and her grown-up boyfriends
Summon her shape in *Shape* magazine
This is a focus group
This is a granting organization
The inside of a car
An animal is a hurt
Hurt inside your shoulder and thigh
I'm throwing pills over a bridge
Things got as ugly
As cherries on a billboard
I slept on the oily river and watched the fires
No one chose me
Particularly the world sunning its muscle on the lawn
Speaking as a gladiator
I felt fine
The falcons and hawks
The solo roadrunner
Dropped mice blithely into the pool
Their ghosts blotted out the steam shovels
Mile by mile
We dusk

Little Elegy (Eros)

Women in my generation

Never say cunt

Tonight I read

Two poems by two oh—10 years older?—

One says hers is a tree with a mouth

The other says hers is a mind from "lip to cunt to bone."

Wow!

And once, I overheard: "Cunt!" of another

Woman who had betrayed Her.

The C is hard and critical,

The C that begins my name.

No tree

No heart, no bone

No sister enemies

No source or power

In the middle of me,

Though sometimes, something true,

Which is *agape*

     & the color blue

Once, a beautiful boy, blinking and new

Born young and old

Inclined to obedience without cause

Is it? Are you my mother?

Said the baby bird to the bulldozer

Hatchlings   this glorious orphanhood!

Little Elegy (Eve)

Women of my generation don't say joy

Playing with (t)he (i)r happiness

Yes, what was deemed love was a game

Jouisssance inside decades then gone

I loved me

With less joy

(*joi*)

In my arms

Before—one yelp—I wandered

Into the next

Came a reckoning

Large you know, with legs

And belts that tied down

Such a prior proud animal

"She looks, you know,

Like a feral thing now, so you see

How it is, I can't touch her."

Such a winnowing

For a born before widow!

Les Demoiselles D'Avignon, The Bride Stripped Bare by Her
Bachelors Even,

You decided early in the 21st to stop aiding the 20th

Oh Miss Margaret Jarvis, oh Kiki,

Gone, POOF!!!

Summoning a new shape

Bereft at last of beauty and her stupid brother, *Monsieur Bricollage*,

If you ever call me a method again—

Oulipo, Oulipo, all the way home . . .

Yes I loved me until she was gone

Joyeux   Joyeux   Joyeux Noël

Pity Boat

I would not blow
           Into the tube
Of the life vest
Not in English
Nyet in Spanish
There were far too many ways to drown
Flying over Texas

           So I'm lying
Next to William Blake
In a big rubber raft
& he's teaching me how to love
Being dead. A slow study,
I fling my arms
After every cactus we pass.
"You're dumb, Claudia," Blake says.
"I am not," I say and poke
Poor William Blake
With a gun.
William Blake is beyond asking why.
And since the many and/or the few
Fuck everyone and/or thing they can
& since to fuck is to hit with a club,
He moved to Paradise.
I drive each day
Down Paradise Road
& one day I saw myself there.
I was 11 and I was crying
Running home through eucalyptus
To the *El Granada* motel.
Those trees knew the future,
Sweet tan bark
Shedding perpetually
In the salty air.
William Blake stretches out,
Happily naked and dead
In the what's next.
He's a singing a song behind my eyelids
Somebody knows where we're going
William Blake is eating stars
& one, very slowly,
Brightens inside my mouth

Mary Wasn't Sure

Mary wasn't sure about any of it. She didn't like her traveling cloak and she didn't like the donkey.

She didn't like the manger, or the shit that had lodged
itself on her shoe.

She didn't like the Kings and their smelly gifts.

She'd liked paying her taxes, and the sharp clatter the coins made when counted, though she hadn't liked the journey, none of it, or all the new villages one after the other withholding all the stories she'd never hear or tell. She really didn't like the donkey who kept turning its head and nipping her ankles. And she hated her traveling cloak.

She liked the angels and their sexlessness. Their vacant smiles
so full of promise. The sudden hope she felt when
they played their golden horns.

She wondered if she was an angel, but no, she had a baby. He lay in a manger, no crib for his bed.

She liked the baby, its helplessness. His name was Jesus.
She wondered if he was an angel, but no, he was a baby. They, neither of them, were angels. They were in it together, first of all the manger, and then all the rest of the story both she and Jesus already knew. The shepherds, too. They knew and they liked the baby who lay on her traveling cloak on the straw.

She didn't like the story, except the beginning, she didn't like the way she knew how it was going to end, not because she already, as Jesus already, knew the end, but because it was a tragedy, and she didn't like tragedies. No one would remember this, the small and smelly manger and the helpless baby who was clean and eating, who lay in her traveling cloak on the straw. No one would remember her as she was now, a girl who'd just paid her taxes and had a baby she called Jesus, who she'd bathed in a trough and lay in her cloak on the straw. She was a girl who'd just had a baby, she was happy, if a little tired, and Jesus was happy, if asleep, but no one would paint this picture enough. No, she saw it all, she knew it all already, and so did Jesus in his baby sleep, dreaming himself the dead man his mother would hold forever in her lap.

Little Elegy (Vietnam)

The general is dead,

Who said we didn't lose.

The general was a humanist:

Kill more, he knew,

And they'd have to surrender.

But the further East,

Westmoreland,

Whole villages and families napalmed,

The further lost,

He and his war became.

The general was a humanist:

Scratching his head

On his last day

Wondering why, though he killed so many,

The East to the

West

Gave not one bit

More land.

Little Elegy (Mary Mulvaney Vitali)

I wanted a life, a poem

Of many places, words

At a time,

& I have one.

Waking to research the truck,

I find the Gettysburg Address

In its open back

& my stray childhood, too.

We were equal there,

Shoulders pressed against the warm metal,

Split almost directly in half

Those of us who would die young:

Danny, in his parents' basement,

& Pat Fallon hung from a rope.

I'm alive and Michael, too.

Riding today on Highway 101

I'm in the eucalyptus' smell

1971, my knees a tangle of other knees,

Mr. and Mrs. Vitali smoking cigarettes in the cab.

Mary Mulvaney dying today, 2002, in Pioneer, California.

I hold her hand there.

I wanted a life a poem

Free in many places,

And dying even now,

I have one.

Little Elegy (At the Orleans)

Without his plural

RIGHTEOUS BROTHER

NOV. 11-16

Is epitaph

He's lost

That loving feeling

Oh, oh, that loving

Feeling

His S, his other,

How much right was His

The Brother

Who is gone

Gone, gone

Oh oh whoah-oh-ah.

Little Elegy (desert to Deseret)

No Moses in a reedy basket,

Your kind of Reid, Harry,

Was made for rods and election,

The slender thread of your voice

Made to calm the Egyptians.

Give a ladder to that Latter-Day!

I was born on Nevada day,

So every year share my birth

With government workers

Who frolic in the cactus

As we watch another missile

Implode over Mt's Edge . . .

I'm hearing the dark Pluto

In the plutonium with our name on it,

I'm searching for reeds in the desert,

And nearby our children play in the newest gravel pit.

Here's our book, Harry, so please, please,

Read!

Little Elegy (American Justice)

The Banker's family

Was awarded

More than the Fireman's

& the Stockbroker's

More than the Cop's

The Insurance Man

Won out too, over

The small Rosa

Who dusted his many pens,

And all the way down

The many floors, the lives

Were rated, all of those

Who died September 11th.

Little Elegy (New Orleans and Biloxi)

The divinity leaking

    The living lose

Whole cities to force

Leaky Jesus

    Fallen from his human mother

A series of days   All category 3

Depictions of catastrophe

    Pharaoh's drowning army

Strewn beaches after any number

    Of huge waves

The frigidity of the wave in Japanese painting

    & interpretation of blame

The kinetics of every day

Moving through each of us

Self such a small arc in the tapestry

Though the trope of the infant and mother

Pleased me more than the hunt

What I was "about"

    When I was about

Traceable in the journals destroyed

Every one of them, his wife reports in Biloxi,

By a force only fourth

In the record of such force

What is it "about"

When it is about?

Little Elegy (cummingsworth)

I   Loves My Collective

                Uncollective

-ly   whee, whee

                All the way home

Only baby goes home

                & Papa goes

To market & someone

                Else eats meat

Getting & spending etc

                Lay waste

But the five little friends too small

                For the burden

Ease it

                Inside their common nest.

Little Elegy (Kenneth Koch)

I called you tennis coach

Because you were elegant

And I could see you in the white shorts

Swinging a racket blithely back and forth.

You told me

That Alice Notely told you

She believed poetry

Was the most important thing in the world

& when I said it is

You asked: "More important than brain surgery?"

We sat together as guests in Iowa

And when you wondered aloud why

It took us so long to meet

I heard the echo of your line resound

Through the hearts of thousands.

Little Elegy (Robert Creeley)

Here can't recognize

There, thought it moves

Inside it,

And I can't find

You in your poems.

Nothing whatsoever

Of love, love of God,

God love, love or God,

In a Pope.

It's the lack

That teaches.

Look, he's over

She's there, there . . .

I never touched your empty eye place,

Everything all spilled from it.

The shape of you,

A shape that's filled with the waiting

You gave off, sometimes

More patiently than others,

Is patiently beside me,

Or in me, or both,

Right now.

You are not an elsewhere!

Passing through me

Passing through you

Though I'm solid,

I'm a passenger

On an airplane.

There's no You to visit,

But you do.

Little Elegy Unsung

Said   good-bye   to a way

      Via age & the end

Of My U.S.

      The notes don't sound in the spaces

Don't drop into place

      In the Beloved Plurality

Where did you

      Go wrong

This way

      & that
Here

      & There

Green, green

      Absorbed in flags

And a way waylaid

I dreamt we ripped up the grass

And laid carpet over the earth

The heat came   The carpet died

"We certainly weren't doing anybody any favors"

"& He certainly wasn't doing her any favor . . ."

Our day was   out of favor

& this was *my* Mojave

II. What is Meant Here By the People

Finally Don Quixote understood her problem: she was both a woman (sic.) therefore she couldn't feel love and a knight in search of Love. She had to become a knight, for she could solve this problem only by becoming partly male.

—Kathy Acker

What is Meant Here By the People

Problem with   "knowledge" including

    "Know how"   including   "knowing how to live"

What is meant here by   "the people"

And who is one

What is meant here by the people and how to become one

I carried the heavy child across the river

I knew how   I meant to be a child

Including knowing how to live

And forgetting the lesser know how

What is meant here by the child

Excludes the possibility of the people

However well you know one

I know one

There is more

The river the currency   carried this child in me

Carried this knowing how to live

And was one

The Sister Worlds (Antigone)

1.

The series of unkindnesses grew,
The series behind the unkindness kindled and undressed.
I'm a number lost my zero when I didn't bury brother
Verily alright—
Verily and verily a series a kindness and number—
Brother brother our deaths were the end of the series.
Butt in the air, she's on her knees—
The world says she wants it—
She says she wants it—
All to disappear.
But she's on her knees,
She's on her knees in a series,
Of billboards, a red one
A brown one, a lolly
Verily and hither,
All in one
Two, three,   you're out!
Magna cum Body
Graduating and bare
Under the starlight

                    (lover true no less to Beloved are you)
2.

Under your umbrella
Are you my mother?
Under your umbrella
On Industry Rd.
Instead of Zimbabwe,
Are you my mother?
Slumped in your shopping cart
My brother lies buried,
My serial brother, my love, my ethic
Buried in your shopping cart,
Is she not real ("are you true?")
Is he less dead,
Buried in a shopping cart,
A trash can as serial girls
One and two

Buried by serial son
Of serial father jailed in Oregon?

Signal the bulldozer
Speed thy song

Grand Theft Auto

My little car-thief plans with his face
And with his heart and from his hand
Come children and their children.

He wins the game!
Choosing each time to crash
& not to kill

He springs up from the remote

Control

To kiss me, standing alone
Listening to birds

Representation Without Taxation

A meadow full of Easter lilies

Turned into a province on a map,

The province renamed 20 times in 20 years.

In The Tiger Information Center, Asia lies sleeping . . .

Being here/or there/and how it feels,

And how I say my name to you

As in "I am not your Lily,"

Or "A meadow is finally only a province-in-progress . . ."

Ask any tiger,

But don't ask me, I'll only try to make you love me.

So many nation-states in a name!

I was surprised, were you?

"Our" identity problem,

Is it clinical or critical?

Haven't they made a government yet,

Who's gone to exile this week?

His wife needs us to deposit some money,

She who was the jewel chick of Liberia . . .

Liberia! So surprised to get her letter

I wrote and sent her the Key to *Uncle Tom's Cabin.*

Every place that ends in *eria* is the Key to exile,

And some are cold and some hot on their enforced Isle.

And we, we are the hot air ballooning above you . . .

About Suffering They Were

I believed the linguist

On the radio who said words are most interesting

When they indicate something not there,

Something not inherently in or of themselves.

Freud thought of writing as the voice of an absent person.

I miss my father, and though I see signs,

I've begun to forget the sound of his voice.

So the roads come after, not before, which puzzled

The Japanese tourists on the architectural tour

In Harvard Square. Mercy, therefore, is made.

A Baedeker to follow, in any missing language.

A little embarrassing after all that no, there's nobody here

And her form too is continual instruction.

The new poem is the old master's painting.

Manifest suffering in every time zone

While father, as he must, goes elsewhere.

The old poem . . . There are no old poems,

Only new textbooks directing

The unprepared student to the painting

Behind the poem. I believed the phonetist,

Waking one day at last lost in the vowels

Of her dreaming.

Sleep me there.

The new poem is the sound

In the old master's painting.

We'll be tortured there,

Along with the animals

Whose suffering is mute

Or written in our missing language.

Father. Inconsequential me.

The feathers in our death.

Falling into yours.

$$\frac{42}{43}$$

III. Everybody's Autobiography

Not in Utopia, — subterranean fields, —
Or some secreted island, Heaven knows where!
But in the very world, which is the world
Of all of us, — the place where in the end
We find our happiness, or not at all!

—William Wordsworth

Claudia Keelan

Everybody's Autobiography

1.

At the end, the only thing left in my parents' house was the piano
and an oversized portrait of them on their wedding day.
At the end, he died in my house, in Las Vegas, and I called *I love you Dad*

through moments struck open, a lid on a trunk that was our life together,
struck open, in his dying. At the end, the firemen and paramedics,
the coroner from Chicago smoking on the porch, and the captain saying

would you like to pray? At the end, we did, struck open, the bed
that was his tomb still in the guest room, and yet no angel telling me
of the risen Lord. At the end, I kept returning to the room

to look at my father. In the end, they placed him in a bag, I heard
the zipping and though I didn't watch, I heard the effort they made lifting,
and he was gone, no sirens, before my son woke.

2.

In the beginning, in 1924, Lenin died, and Stalin ruled for 29 years.
Calvin Coolidge was president and there was no vice-president.
Clarence Darrow, a man who, unlike my father, believed in law, helped
Leopold and Loeb to escape the death penalty for the murder
of their 14-year-old cousin.

In the beginning, Ruth Malcomson from Pennsylvania was named
Miss America, and George Gershwin's *Rhapsody in Blue*
debuted in Paris.

On April 3rd, 1924, my father Edward Thomas Keelan Jr., was born
in Compton, California to Marguerite Keelan *nee* Kearns and Edward
Thomas Keelan Sr., the boy between two girls, Peggy 2 and Patricia
the baby. This is the autobiography of everyone because all lives
and books begin and end.

This is the autobiography of everyone
and is for all of us still alive in the broken middleness,

mouthing our stories.
My father fell into this world from a woman's body.
And yours?
This is the autobiography of everyone
Because it was my father who taught me to distrust
distinctions that separated the simple subject from
the compound subject, particularly, and to begin with,
the subject I. *I'm hungry*, I told my father.

The world is rumbling he said,
and placed a piece of bread in my mouth.
I'm thirsty, I repeated and he pointed towards the split in the dream
and handed me a hollow stick.

3.

Of death, Gertrude Stein writes in *The Geographical History of America:*

> Now the relation of human nature is this.
> Human nature does not know this.
> Human nature cannot know this . . .
> Human nature does not know that if everyone did not die
> There would be no room for those who live now.

This is true. Almost everything that Stein said was true.
I know because I've felt it happen, human nature.
Human nature is interested in itself.
One day, human nature finds a place—a room, a table, a field, a site
of becoming—where human nature loses, in a flash, first distinction,
and finds itself suddenly something other,
one's whole understanding of a glorious singularity
disappeared in an instant.

How large the world has become in your loss!
You have understood the purpose of death.
Having done so, you understand the purpose of life.
You must give your self away. Then you can sleep.

Stein: "This is the way human nature can sleep, it can sleep by not
knowing this. The human mind can sleep by knowing this."
I have spent my life asleep,
standing by the window year after year with my mother,
waiting for my father to come home safely.
This is the autobiography of everyone
asleep in one room or the other.
Natural mind, have you seen my father?

4.

In the beginning, Walt Disney created his first cartoon and another invention, the Teapot Dome Scandal, debuted in Wyoming, and Elk Hills, California, not far from where my father worked the oil wells years later.

Harry F. Sinclair of Sinclair Oil Company was sentenced to prison
for contempt of the Senate and for hiring detectives to shadow members of
the jury in his case.

I liked the dinosaur in the Sinclair oil sign, just as I found
the oil wells themselves, perpetually making love
to the edges of Interstate 5, oddly comforting,
though a little sad.

In the years before my father was born, the Southern Pacific Railroad
monopolized California. William Hood was the chief assistant
engineer who saw that tunnels were the only clear route through
the sometimes impenetrable mountains.

He envisaged eighteen tunnels in twenty-eight miles of track
climbing down the Tehachapi Mountain to the San Joaquin Valley
below. The Southern Pacific Railroad was as merciless as it was
inventive. When a town denied access to the company,
it simply built another town.

The farmers too felt the brunt of the railroad's power.
Allowed to settle on isolated land, in Tehachapi, in Boron
and many desert regions of the state, many farmers had cultivated
the barren land into lush fields.

5.

In 1878, the Southern Pacific Railroad took titles to the land and
appraised the land at twenty-five to fifty dollars, instead of the two
dollars and fifty cents originally quoted the farmers.
Outraged, they went to court where they lost every case.

By the end, eight farmers died and two hundred families were
evicted from their farms. Earlier, in 1881, the Southern Pacific
joined the Atchison, Topeka and *Sante Fe* Railroad at Deming
in New Mexico territory to become the second transcontinental
    railroad.

My parents sang the song as we drove along, and so did we,
along with "I've Been Working on the Railroad," "Give me a Ticket
for an Airplane," wanting I suppose now that I think of it,
to be anywhere but the car.

For all their invention and cruelty, the founders of the railroad
obviously had a vision of shared beauty built into their machine.
The dining cars of the early railroads were elegant meeting places
where travelers met over fine china, eating roast pheasant, exotic

relishes and drinking California wine as they gamboled together
towards different destinations. The gilded age of the railroad ended
in 1910 when Hiram Johnson was elected governor of California
and methodically broke the political hold

of the Southern Pacific Railroad. A United States senator
from 1917-1945, Johnson was the Progressive party's
nominee for vice-president in 1912.

6.

As a senator, he was an isolationist, opposing membership
to the League of Nations and the United Nations. A large state
on the edge of the Pacific, California itself is contained, isolated,
and like all things in isolation, it has no concept of boundaries.

Apotheosis of the "bedroom community," the suburbs
of Southern California are predicted in the next century
to reach Las Vegas. The golden state, *El Dorado*, California
was the destination dream spot of millions of immigrants

from the 1800's when pioneers traveled the California-Oregon
trail, to the present day when Mexican émigrés are smuggled
across the border, camouflaged as part of the car's seat.

It can be no mistake that in the years during Johnson's
political career, the oil companies laid the foundation for
the state's eventual enslavement to the gasoline combustion engine.

With the downfall of the Southern Pacific Railroad,
the oil barons took, and continue to hold, the transportation
realities of the multitude of Californians who now inhabit

El Dorado, alone, or commuting, and mostly in traffic jams,
in automobiles along the state's freeways.

7.

A Brief History of the Major Oil Companies in the Gulf Region

1889: Standard Oil (Indiana) founded as subsidiary of Standard Oil Trust

1911: Standard Oil of Indiana founded with the dissolution of Standard Oil

1910: Standard Oil of Indiana purchases Pan American Petroleum

1932: Standard Oil of Indiana sells Venezuela operation to Jersey

1954: Pan American and Standard of Indiana merge, new company is called American Oil Company [Amoco]

1957: Begins joint venture with Iran independent of Iranian Oil Consortium

1959: Amoco signs agreements with Shah of Iran

1959: Jersey strikes oil in Libya

1972: Jersey changes name to Exxon

1972: Saudi Arabia, Abu Dhabi, Kuwait and Quatar acquired 25% interest in Exxon's production operations (in country), with right to increase stake to 51% by 1982

1981: Exxon sells Standard Libya to Libyan government. Along with Amoco, Getty, Exxon, Ashland Oil, Chevron, Conoco and many others continue to operate in the Gulf Region. The Exxon company acquiring interest there in 1928, in the Turkish, (now Iraq) Petroleum Co.

8.

My father died on July 21st, 2001, and on September 11th, 2001,
eleven boys in four airplanes crashed into the World Trade Center,
the Pentagon, and into a field in Pennsylvania,
killing themselves and thousands of people.

This has something to do with my father, with oil, with me.
My government and with you.

Since my father's death, I've slowly begun waking to my childhood.
It's mostly full of other people's words, as is time in general, the specific
a rare event, relying as it does upon an individual member being awake.

I'm waking to my childhood in my own child's life,
the driving he loves on video games, a version of the driving I loved, asleep
in the backseat. May all his crashing be virtual.

In remembering is re-membering.
Heart and mind, body and soul, time and space, father and daughter,
we are separate; we are attached.

The mind knows this when the heart pulses freely,
dependent on its own muscle.
The soul itself is a muscle, both housed
and independent of its own body.

I'm aware of its contraction now, in the arc its making outside me
as it follows the automobile's whine, which is a pulse too, surrounding
each moment of modern life.

Time is eternal in space. Trapped radio waves prove it,
as does my dead father's DNA wound through me.

Heaven, then, spirals in a dragon fly's hovering, look, just now,
and in its vanishing.

IV. Bildung Sequence

I'm your desire's object, dog, because I can't be the subject. Because I can't be the subject: What you name "love," I name "nothingness." I won't not be: I'll perceive and I'll speak.

—Kathy Acker from *Don Quixote*

Bildung Sequence

1.

The parade of bodies
The parade of bodies   In the waiting room
On the sidewalk I see them
Attending their x-rays   worried over the sugar count
And two who agree killing him would be best
Walking here in the bright desert light
A shadow with shadows
Two feet, four, six feet
Footsteps over footsteps walking through dust
My dead father passing on the left
A living man in the same purple jacket
Right hip slightly lifted like his
Walking through dust
In the bright desert light a shadow with others
In the dust in the fumes
I've begun to remember
My first self
She wanted so much
"Who is the third who walks always beside you?"
Who is she? To whom does she belong?
In the tree is a figure of a man
He has legs and is living
Below the tree the bodies parade
He has legs and a third
"And if the body does not do fully as much as the soul?
"And if the body were not the soul, what is the soul?"
Not discerning their faces, but describing
Not feeling the flesh but feeling
"Who is the third who walks always beside you?"
A shadow inside flesh
A shadow proving your face temporary
A part I have wanted to celebrate
"Here is no water but only rock/Rock and no water and the sandy road"
You take the Low Ghost and I'll take the High Ghost
"The simple, compact, well-join'd scheme, myself disintegrated
Every one disintegrated yet part of the scheme . . ."

A man in a tree sees horse
Two legs, three, seven
Footsteps inside of footsteps
They put me in a coat so the x-ray would not hurt anything living
　　　　　　inside me
Bright desert light　　　　　x-rays
All that's left uncounted

2. Little Elegy (Ground Zero)

"A crowd flowed over, so many,
I had not thought death had undone so many . . ."
The one I know, nowhere near
& the others, the fire from the plane's
Crash so hot, they clasped
Hands and stepped
Off the broken tower,
Their falling, a choice they made as one:

". . . THE PALE, POWDER-LIGHT, POWDER-DRY DUST OF AUGUST
FROM WHICH THE LONG WEEK'S MARKS OF HOOF AND WHEEL . . .
WITH SOMEWHERE BENEATH THEM, VANISHED BUT NOT GONE, FIXED
AND HELD IN THE UNNANNEALING DUST, THE NARROW, SPLAYED
TOES PRINTS OF HIS WIFE'S BARE FEET; HIS OWN PRINTS, HIS OWN
PRINTS SETTING THE PERIOD NOW AS HE STRODE . . . HIS BODY
BREAKING THE AIR HER BODY HAD VACATED, HIS EYES TOUCHING
THE OBJECTS—POST AND TREE AND FIELD AND HOUSE AND HILL—
HER EYES HAD LOST . . ."

Go Down Moses, I say go down
All writing an elegy for the living,
Putting pictures in photo albums,
Bringing the trash dutifully to the curb . . .
Nothing gets free of this world.
The glum angels in Wim Wender's *Wings of Desire*,
What are the words in German for the tired book?
Bildung Roman? World-weary and yet
There they are, the angels, looking over
Your shoulder in the library, mouthing along
With the words . . .
"When you want me again, look for me under . . ."
I threw a book on the scorpion.
Its death was all over the cover . . .
Was it performative or normative,
The subject's death I mean?
"One is not involved in the conception
Of the airplane, nor its invention,
But one can very well

Steer the flying machine, and de-turn
Its usage . . ."
Not manna, but the last man and woman,
Hands clasped, falling from the sky,
The Fall itself free from metaphor at last in the reply,
A man and woman in business suits,
Choosing their means of dying,
Living to the last in air
Instead of fire.

3. Little Elegy (Imagination)

The unseen is not a shadow world,
A better parody of here . . .
"One must have a mind of winter . . ."
The old mistake.
"And have been cold a long time . . ."
Gottfried Behn's "cold egotistical eye,"
& other mistakes of Romanticism.
Sasha, the world is real
And imagination too, in generation . . .
"Rooted they/grip down and begin to awaken . . ."
Nothing doesn't exist!
Feathers float down
Around a bird's still body.
My father's ashes
Lie in box headed for Missouri.
Some day, we will scatter him and my mother...
"Look for me under . . ." etc.
The ashes of the 3,000 dead still
There in New York . . .
A starting point.

V. Missing Her

Harriet   *(Singing)*

I dreamed I climbed upon a cliff,
My sister's hand in mine.
Then searched the valley for my house
But only sunny fields could see
And the church spire shining.
I searched until my heart was cold
But only sunny field could see
And the church spire shining.
A girl ran down the mountainside
With bluebells in her hat.
I asked the valley for her name
But only wind and rain could hear
And the church bell tolling.
I asked until my lips were cold
But wakened not yet knowing
If the name she bore was my sister's name
Or if it was my own

—Jane Bowles, from *A Quarreling Pair*

Tide Table

1.

Shall not start with the sea

Though he looks to it,

The man, falling lower and deeper

Into his body as he sits

On a South African shore,

But with the sad pat

A woman sitting beside him

Gives his hand.

        Consolation doesn't involve courage,

Only simple observation:

        History has shrunk him,

The little man,

        To a lonely individual sitting

By the sea.

        Though the water

Unfolds into a narrative of the missing

& is beautiful, the waves

Turn into another man in a hospital bed,

Surrounded by figures whose postures seem friendly,

& then into an angry crowd

Throwing snowballs at a militia.

The individual is left alone by an empty bed

After carrying his father's body

Back to the water where he found him.

2.

Earlier, his chair was empty

     Set at a distance from a row

Of small beach houses. The hotel

     Is the protagonist, function

Is the protagonist and the individual

     Stares through binoculars

On a balcony above

     At three generals who stare

Through binoculars, at the sea,

     Which is filling now, as it always

Fills, with a baptismal party lowering

     An initiate into the water.

The cows that have come to the shore's edge

     Are losing flesh and dying.

Their looking gives them possession

     Without power, the generals and the

Man above the scene.

     The hospital beds are multiplying

And filling, and in the ocean,

Someone with the Star of David

On her back stands beside someone else

Who wears a primitive cross

The artist appears to have smeared

Quickly with his thumb.

There is power in the gaze;

It is elegy, the sea's eternal murmur.

The individual has fallen asleep in the chair

And a newspaper slips down across his feet,

Print face down in the sand.

3.

But who is the individual?

A tribute to her younger self?

"I am so sorry. I was supposed to look after you. But along the way,

I made some bad decisions and in the end,

Turned you into me."

4.

The artist wants to believe

He is an individual,

But he continually blends into a group,

As the hotel alone has no function

Without the three generals

And the solo man. The protagonist

Has bled into a primitive pilgrim

Projected on the wall, and so is

After all, a shadow figure,

As is the artist, despite his belief.

Nothing hidden speaks up for him.

And though the individual has fallen

Short, he has multiplied

Into several, now they are doctors,

Around a hospital bed.

They are as unable as the rest of us,

Yet serve a function.

They help us die.

Body of Evidence

1.

She came as grass   She came in the grass   She did not
Ask what is grass *via* grass She was Green
She came in the grass to which
Your men had already lit fire
She did not ask what is grass   *via* grass she was green
     She was that to which your men had already lit fire

And the fire pursuing her   pursuing the grass and burning
Down the village was beautiful
     Typical   typical fire   powerful fire
She had lived before fire
The grass the native grasses she'd fed on and become never
Knowing that change—Human limb, human sex, human decisions
And mistakes—would blend so easily into grass which she'd with
Pleasure become   *Via* grass she was green

And the blunt little villages the small huts and grazing animals
As grass she'd never distinguish
And everything she touched knew

     Her *not* understanding was true
Beautiful unknowing this wholly unnatural unknowing of what
She'd fed on and become
Her muteness, her green and willing greenness

It was a society   A tribunal
And each living thing that had ever fed from her   bled on her
Lay dead in her   in turn was born in her   in the grass
Which *of* her we'd become.

2.

The gods from whom he stole fire were not her gods
She had no gods she was god   As grass she came in us to become
Society forgot her so part of her

And fire brought pain the fire pursuing her though beautiful
Brought pain brought an overness in her we had not known
She had no gods she was God   and as a god

By others was brought pain
Though still she did not ask   What is grass
Via grass she was green
She was grass to which your men lit fire

By others she was brought pain
By others she was made into a character though her role had always
Been *via* green   To become in grass as grass with others
They lit fires

Burned out of her now
We watched the flames   the powerful flames
The gifted fire given to control her
Via green we had become in grass with others

The fires lit burned her out of us now   Now we became characters
Though our role had always been *via* green
To become as grass with her
We watched the fires separate our bodies we watched
The fire removes us from her.

3.

From becoming came Being which named her which maimed her
And we watched now our mother from far distances
She burned in the rolling flames and as she burnedshe called out our

Names   Far distances cannot explain
We'd become characters   Our role *via* green to burn
Now the names she called into characters   We lit fires
We removed us from her

Named and so forgotten   Society found her missing
Our role via green to burn

Forgot us   We saw her missing everywhere
We could not forget her

Though missing   our names were cells of her
Our role via green to burn
Great holes inside our missing   Her

Same Dream

Each love loved

Taps away at the already

Loved. So I have

Tried to love my first

Self and so she has

Fled me. So I have

Loved only you, Ben,

Until what we became

Opened, and let Lucie in.

Aubade

With no thing prepared   the paradise

    Left us alone in the variety

It was a grave

    The it is a grave

The tried lies in

The next is next

& It is a fine and prosp'rus place

Our whole there   not embraced

Every thing left here

To envy and to love.

Rabbits

Pressed beyond zero   I pressed my ear to her

I found a channel   & radioing   Came a colony

Rousseau's rabbits   A dream of population

      A dream of unpreparing   To prepare

A population of rabbits   I would never see   But dream of

      Forever in my absence from them

In the generation the newest population I and my dream

      Of them   Became her   Then it was I was under

I was below stars   I gave up my dream there

               Under as in beneath

A light so profound a light very possibly streaming

      From a star   Dead already thousands of years

And yet I saw it   So you can see me   As you see her

      As I give up me   For generations   To prepare by

Notes

"What is Meant Here by the People" plays with lines borrowed from Francois Lyotard's book *La Condition Postmoderne: Rapport sur le savoir* (*The Postmodern Condition: A Report on Knowledge*).

"Representation Without Taxation" was written in part as a response to receiving an internet letter request for money from the Jewel Taylor, wife of the exiled president of Liberia, Charles Taylor.

"Bildung Sequence" borrows lines from Fenellosa's essay "The Chinese Written Character as a Medium for Poetry," Whitman's "Song of Myself," Williams' "Spring and All," Eliot's "The Wasteland," Stevens' "The Snowman," and Faulkner's story "Pantaloon in Black" from *Go Down Moses*.

"Everybody's Autobiography" freely adapts information from the Southern Pacific Railroad's official website, and memorials to its history at the Museum of the Southern Pacific Railroad in Sacramento, California.

"Tide Table" is based on painter William Kentridge's interactive work by the same name.

"Body of Evidence" is a translation of the film *The New World* directed by Terrence Malick.

Acknowledgments

Thank you to the following publications where these poems first appeared:

American Letters & Commentary, American Poetry Review, Barrow Street, Cab/Net, The Canary, Cricket-Online Review, Fence, Jacket, The Laurel Review, New American Writing, Packington Review, Parthenon West Review, Quarterly West, Volt, Xantippe

Many thanks also to the editors of *The American Poetry Review* for awarding "Everybody's Autobiography" the 2007 Jerome Shestack prize.

Thanks to my students, friends and family for all their love and faith, and for their own important work.

Photo by Rick Becker-Leckrone

Claudia Keelan is the author of five previous collections of poetry incuding *Refinery, The Secularist, Utopic,* and *The Devotion Field.* Her awards include the Jerome Shestack Award from the *American Poetry Review,* the Beatrice Hawley Award from Alice James Books, the Robert D. Richardson Award from the *Denver Quarterly* and the Silver Pen Award from the State of Nevada. Her poetry has been anthologized in *The Body Electric* (Norton), *American Hybrid* (Norton), *Lyric Postmodernisms* (Counterpath), and *The Book of Irish American Poetry* (University of Notre Dame Press). She lives in Las Vegas with her husband, the poet Donald Revell, and their children Ben and Lucie.

New Issues Poetry

Ruth Ellen Kocher, *When the Moon Knows You're Wandering;*
    One Girl Babylon
Gerry LaFemina, *The Window Facing Winter*
Steve Langan, *Freezing*
Lance Larsen, *Erasable Walls*
David Dodd Lee, *Abrupt Rural; Downsides of Fish Culture*
M.L. Liebler, *The Moon a Box*
Alexander Long, *Vigil*
Deanne Lundin, *The Ginseng Hunter's Notebook*
Barbara Maloutas, *In a Combination of Practices*
Joy Manesiotis, *They Sing to Her Bones*
Sarah Mangold, *Household Mechanics*
Gail Martin, *The Hourglass Heart*
Justin Marks, *A Million in Prizes*
David Marlatt, *A Hog Slaughtering Woman*
Louise Mathias, *Lark Apprentice*
Gretchen Mattox, *Buddha Box, Goodnight Architecture*
Carrie McGath, *Small Murders*
Paula McLain, *Less of Her; Stumble, Gorgeous*
Lydia Melvin, *South of Here*
Sarah Messer, *Bandit Letters*
Wayne Miller, *Only the Senses Sleep*
Malena Mörling, *Ocean Avenue*
Julie Moulds, *The Woman with a Cubed Head*
Carsten René Nielsen, *The World Cut Out with Crooked Scissors*
Marsha de la O, *Black Hope*
C. Mikal Oness, *Water Becomes Bone*
Bradley Paul, *The Obvious*
Jennifer Perrine, *The Body Is No Machine*
Katie Peterson, *This One Tree*
Jon Pineda, *The Translator's Diary*
Donald Platt, *Dirt Angles*
Elizabeth Powell, *The Republic of Self*
Margaret Rabb, *Granite Dives*
Rebecca Reynolds, *Daughter of the Hangnail; The Bovine Two-Step*
Martha Rhodes, *Perfect Disappearance*
Beth Roberts, *Brief Moral History in Blue*
John Rybicki, *Traveling at High Speeds* (expanded second edition)
Mary Ann Samyn, *Inside the Yellow Dress; Purr; Beauty Breaks In*
Ever Saskya, *The Porch is a Journey Different From the House*
Mark Scott, *Tactile Values*
Hugh Seidman, *Somebody Stand Up and Sing*
Heather Sellers, *The Boys I Borrow*
Martha Serpas, *Côte Blanche*

Diane Seuss-Brakeman, *It Blows You Hollow*
Elaine Sexton, *Sleuth; Causeway*
Patty Seyburn, *Hilarity*
Marc Sheehan, *Greatest Hits*
Heidi Lynn Staples, *Guess Can Gallop*
Phillip Sterling, *Mutual Shores*
Angela Sorby, *Distance Learning*
Matthew Thorburn, *Subject to Change*
Russell Thorburn, *Approximate Desire*
Rodney Torreson, *A Breathable Light*
Lee Upton, *Undid in the Land of Undone*
Robert VanderMolen, *Breath*
Martin Walls, *Small Human Detail in Care of National Trust*
Patricia Jabbeh Wesley, *Before the Palm Could Bloom: Poems of Africa*